Contents

Copyright © 2021 by Brunner Studios
All rights reserved. Printed in USA.

All work completed by Brunner Studios

This page left blank for performance purposes.

It Came Upon a Midnight Clear

Sears / Wills

Calmly

3
It
came
u
-
po
-
n
a
mid
-
night
clear,
That
4

6
glor
-
i
-
ous
so
-
ng
of
old.
From
an
-
gels

11
be
-
nd
-
ing
near
the
earth,
to
touch
their
ha
-
rps
of
gold.

Jingle Bells

Brightly

J. Pierpont

3
f
Dash - ing through the snow. In - a one horse o - pen sleigh, O-er the fields we
4

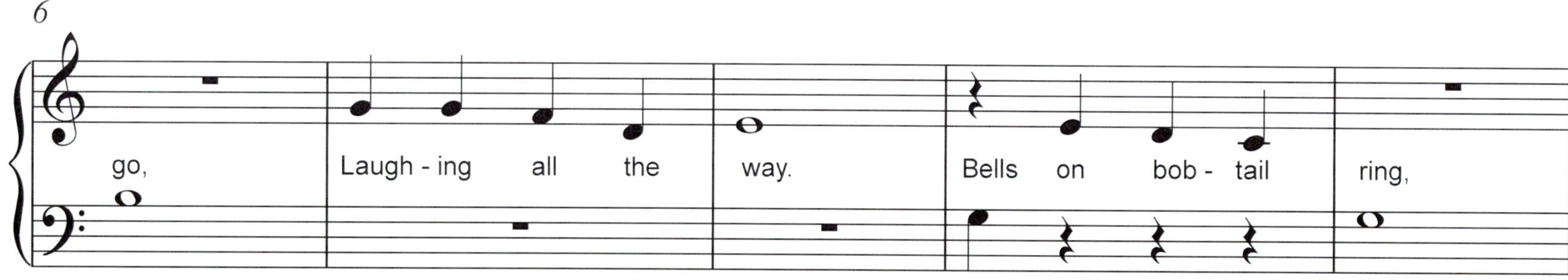
6
go, Laugh - ing all the way. Bells on bob - tail ring,

11
3
mak - ing spir - its bright, What fun it is to laugh and sing a sleigh - ing song to -

16
3
night.
Jing - le bells!
Jing - le bells!
Jing - le all the
way!

21
Oh what fun it
is to ride in - a
one horse op - en
sleigh!
Jing - le Bells!

26
Jing - le bells!
Jing - le all the
way!
Oh what fun it
is to ride in - a

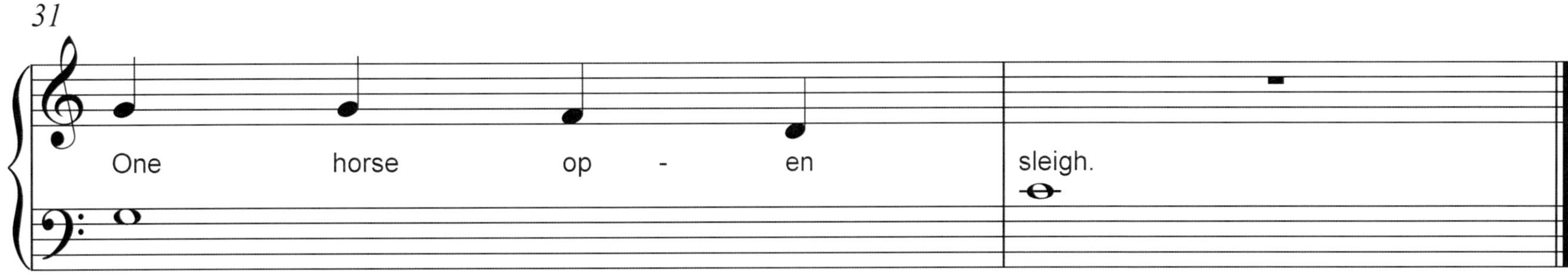
31
One horse op - en
sleigh.

O Come, All Ye Faithful

Boldly

J. F. Wade

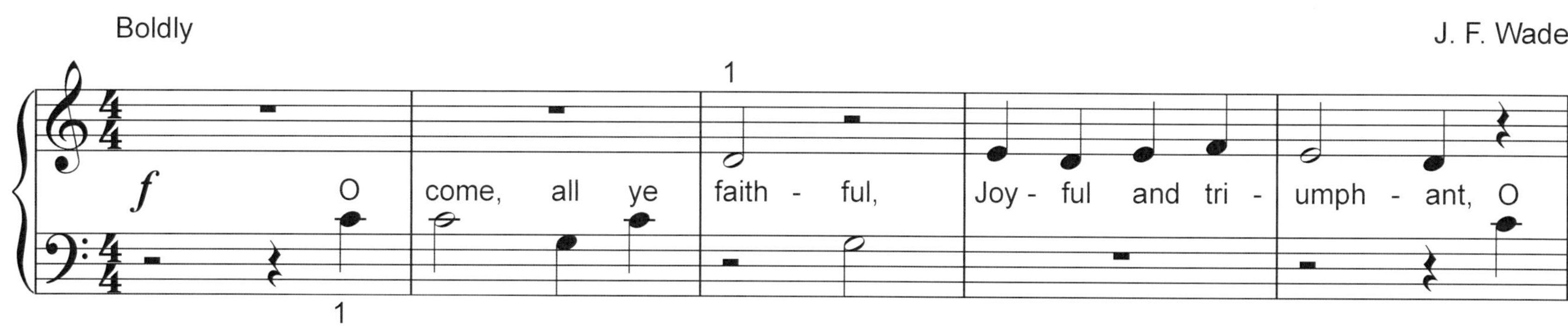
f
1
O
come, all ye
faith - ful,
Joy - ful and tri -
umph - ant, O
1

6
come ye, O
come ye to
Beth - le -
hem.
Come and be -

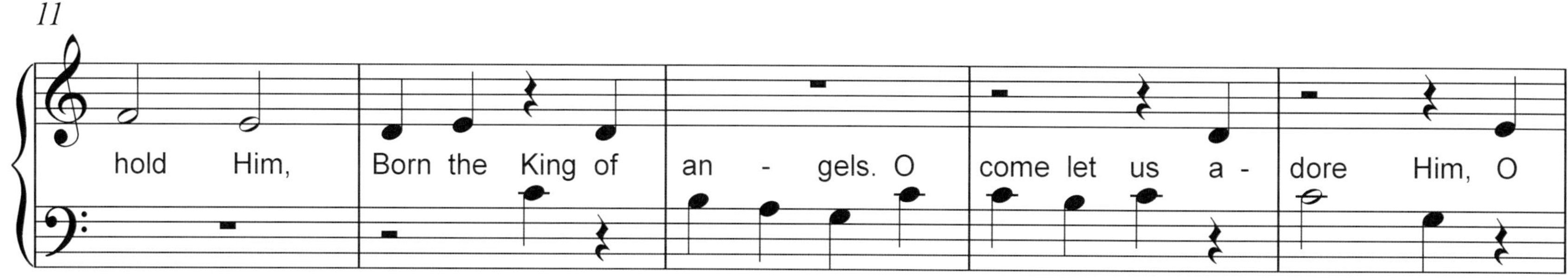
11
hold Him,
Born the King of
an - gels. O
come let us a -
dore Him, O

16
come let us a - dore Him, O come let us a - dore Him, Christ the Lord.

I Saw Three Ships

Traditional

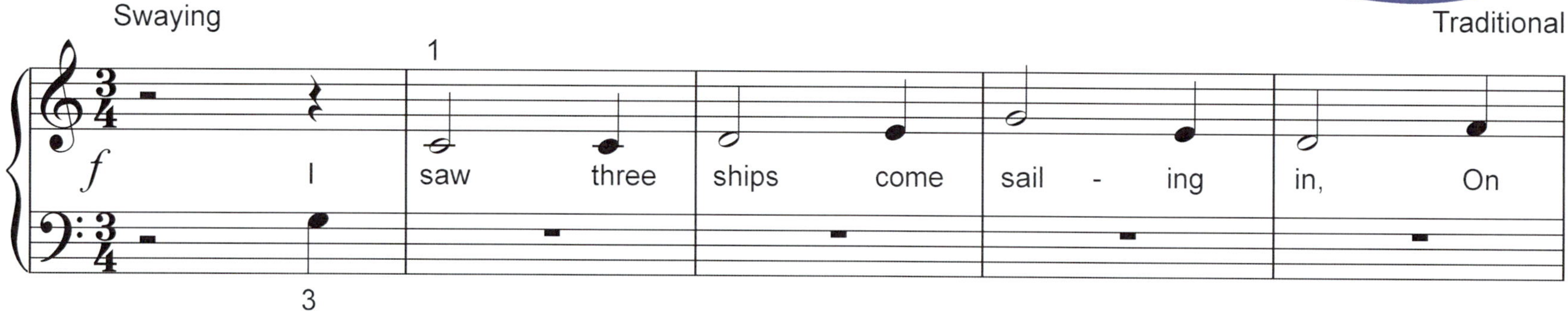
Swaying
1
f
I
saw three ships come sail - ing in, On
3

6
Christ - mas day, on Christ - mas day. I saw three

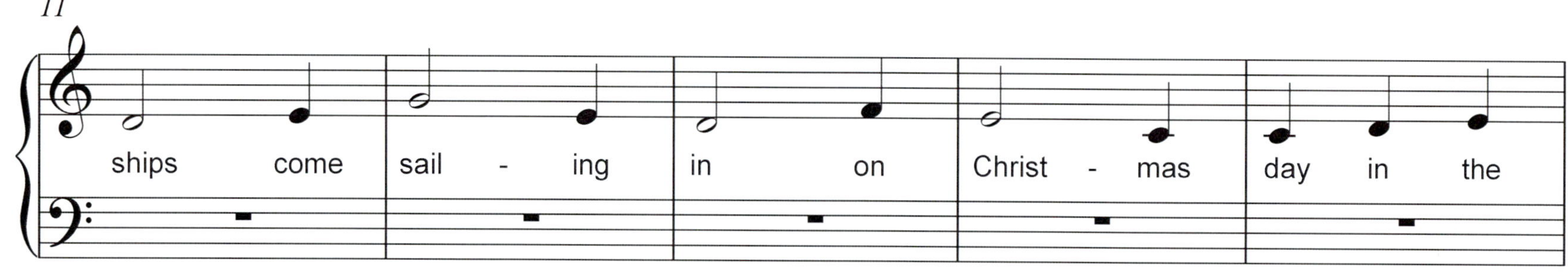
11
ships come sail - ing in on Christ - mas day in the

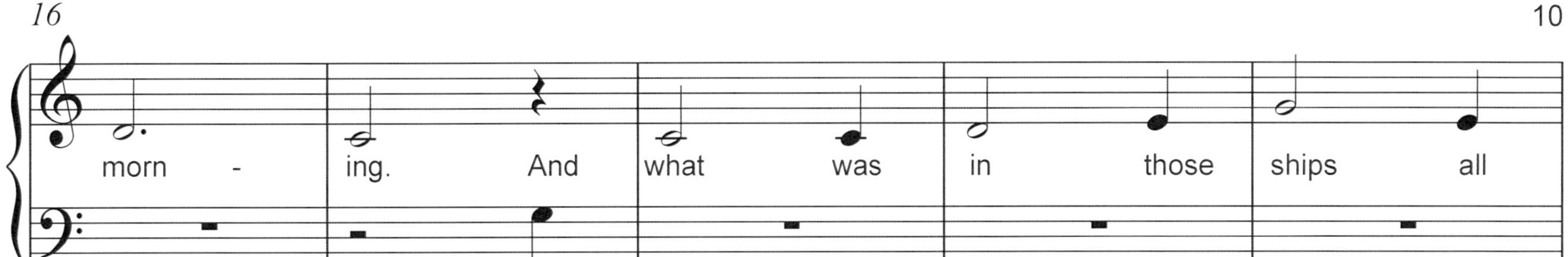
16
morn - ing. And what was in those ships all

21
Three, on Christ - mas day, on Christ - mas day? And

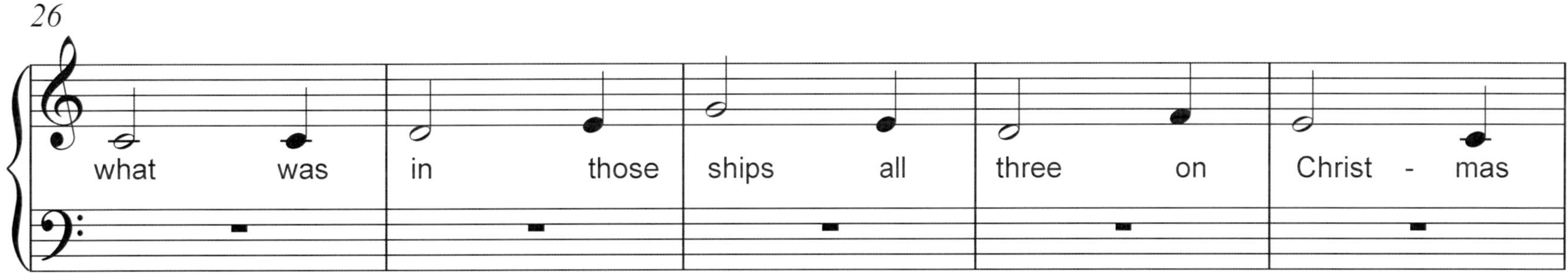
26
what was in those ships all three on Christ - mas

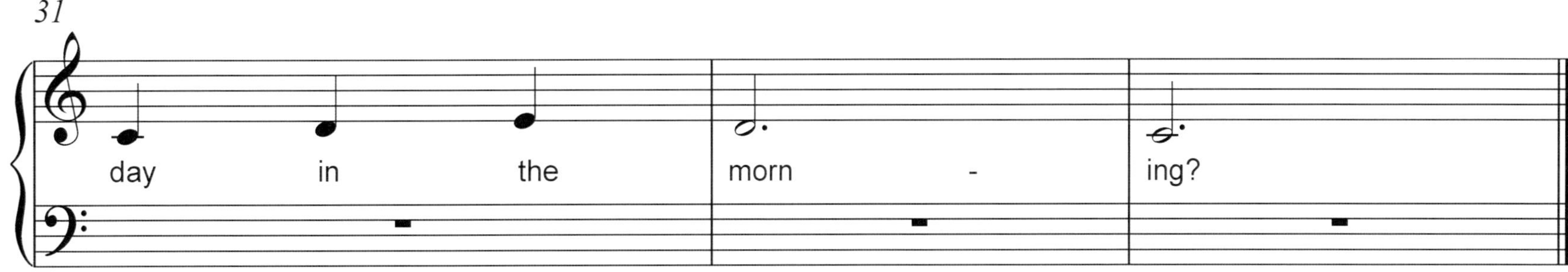
31
day in the morn - ing?

Up on the Housetop

Cheerfully

B. R. Hanby

2
f
Up on the house - top the rein - deer pause; Out jumps
2

6
good old San - ta Claus. Down through the chim - ney with

11
lots of toys, All for the lit - tle ones' Christ - mas

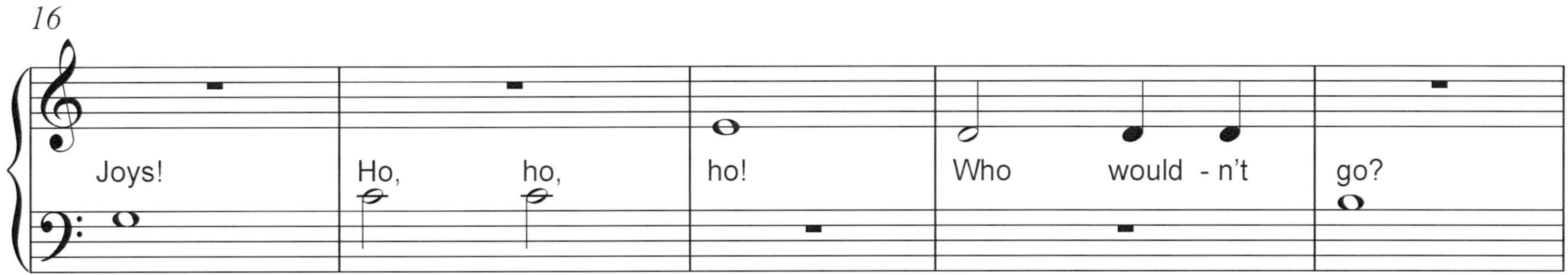
16
Joys!
Ho, ho,
ho!
Who would - n't
go?

21
Ho, ho,
ho!
Who would - n't
go?
Up on the

26
house - top
click, click,
click!
Down through the
chim - ney with

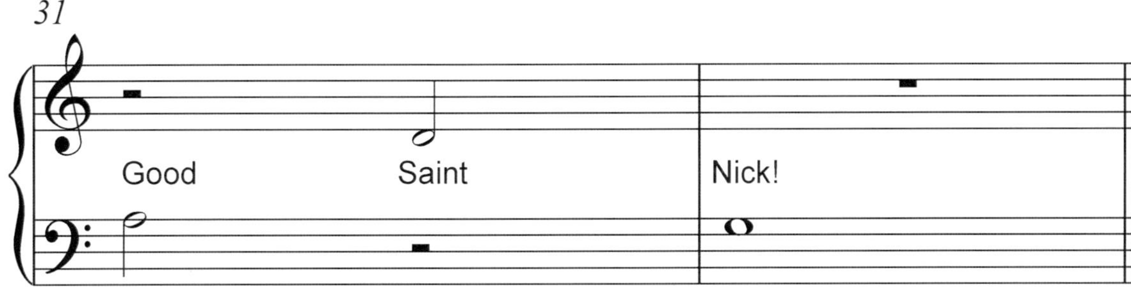
31
Good Saint
Nick!

We Three Kings

Stately

J. H. Hopkins, Jr.

2
f
We three kings of or - i - ent are; bear - ing
1

6
gifts we tra - verse a - far. Field and foun - tain

11
moor and moun - tain, fol - low - ing yon - der star.

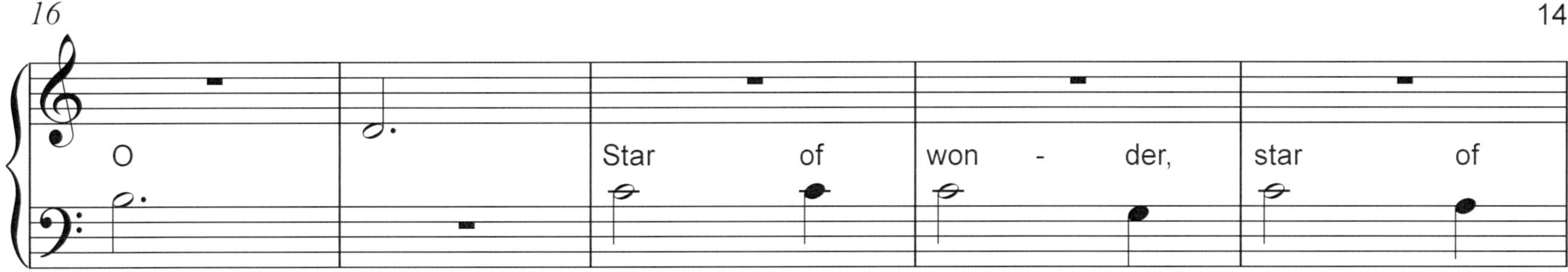
16
O
Star of
won - der,
star of

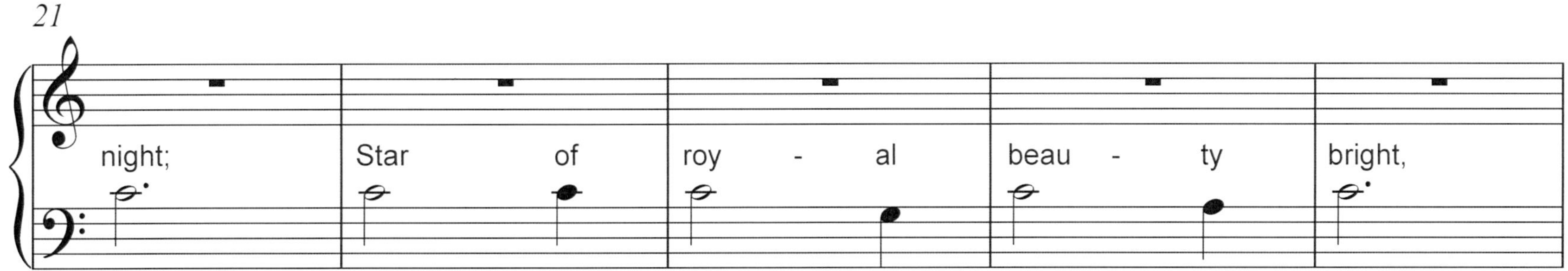
21
night;
Star of
roy - al
beau - ty
bright,

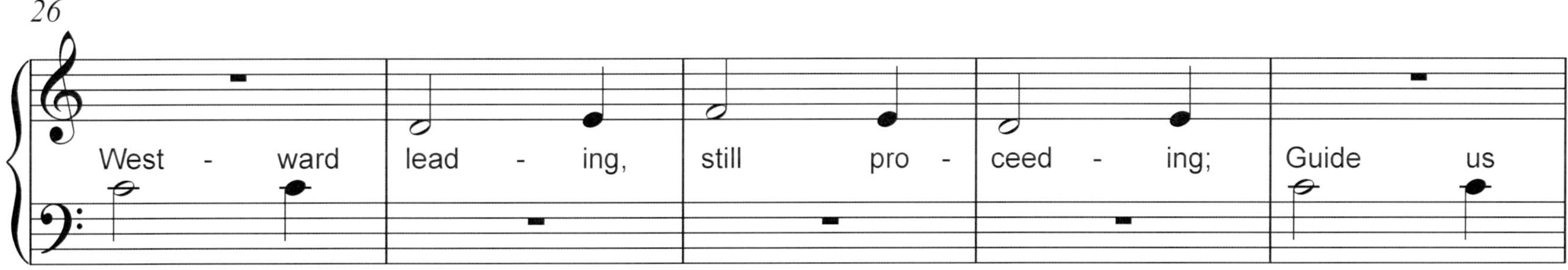
26
West - ward
lead - ing,
still pro -
ceed - ing;
Guide us

31
to Thy
per - fect
light.

Away in a Manger

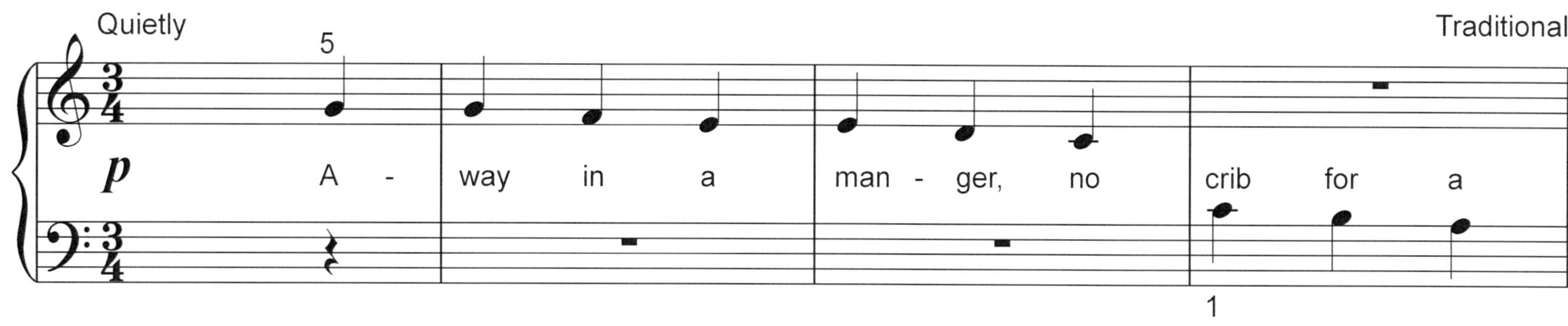
Quietly
Traditional
5
p
A - way in a man - ger, no crib for a
1

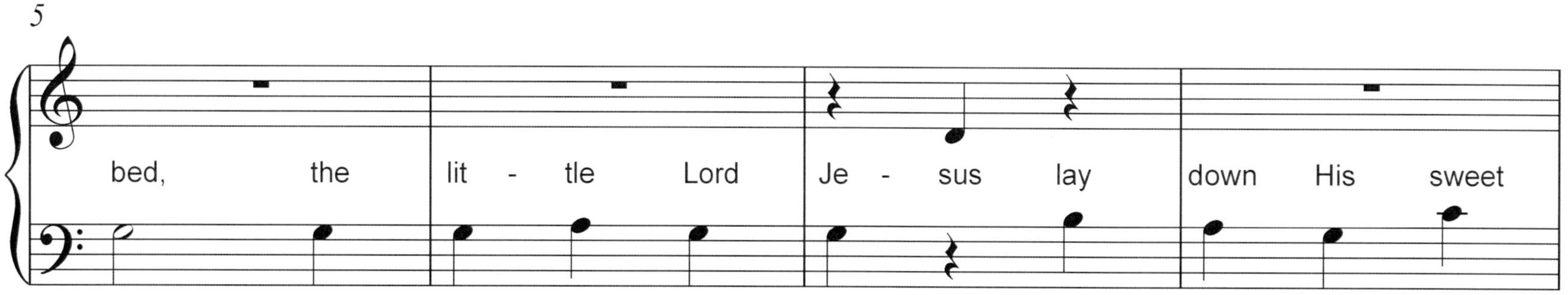
5
bed, the lit - tle Lord Je - sus lay down His sweet

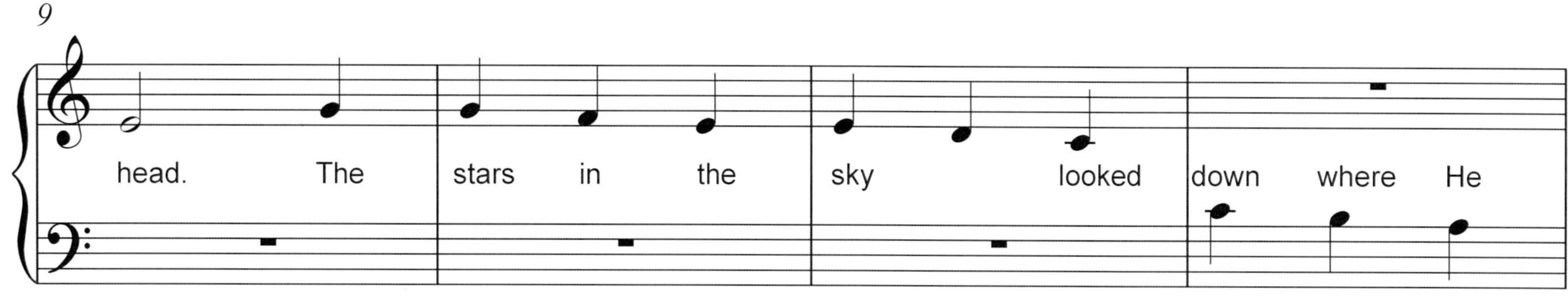
9
head. The stars in the sky looked down where He

13
lay, the lit - tle Lord Je - sus a - sleep on the hay.

List
Sam
Sally
Susan

Jolly Old Saint Nicholas

Happily

Traditional

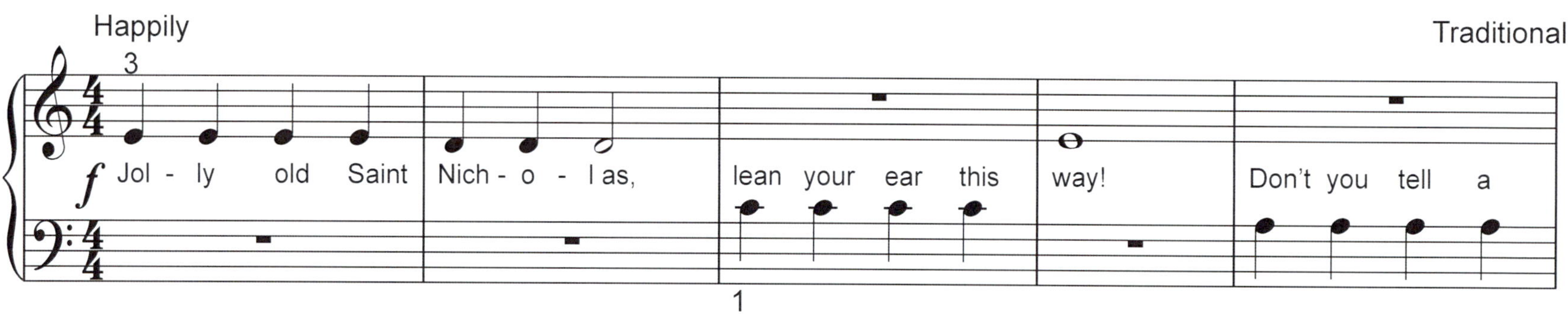
3
f
Jol - ly old Saint
Nich - o - l as,
lean your ear this
way!
Don't you tell a
1

6
sin - gle soul
what I'm going to
say;
Christ - mas Eve is
com - ing soon,

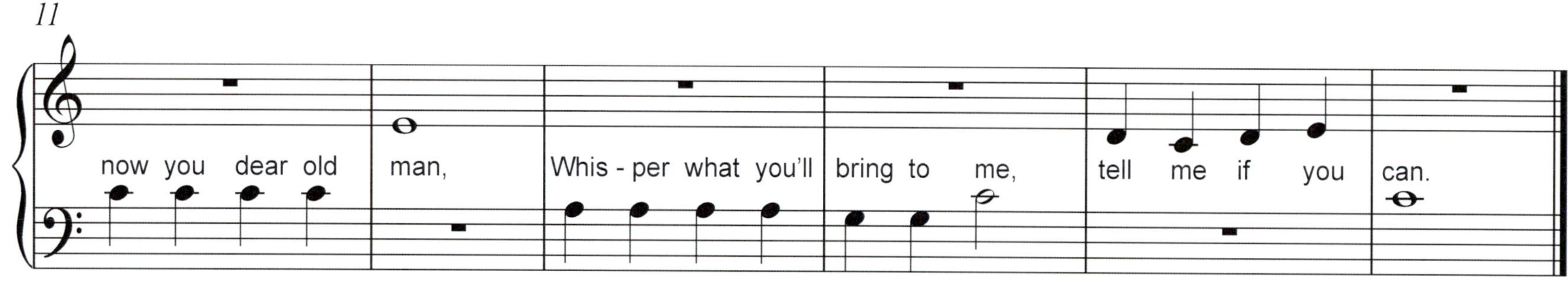
11
now you dear old
man,
Whis - per what you'll
bring to me,
tell me if you
can.

Go Tell It on the Mountain

With motion

Traditional

2
f Go, tell it on the moun - tain, o - ver the
1

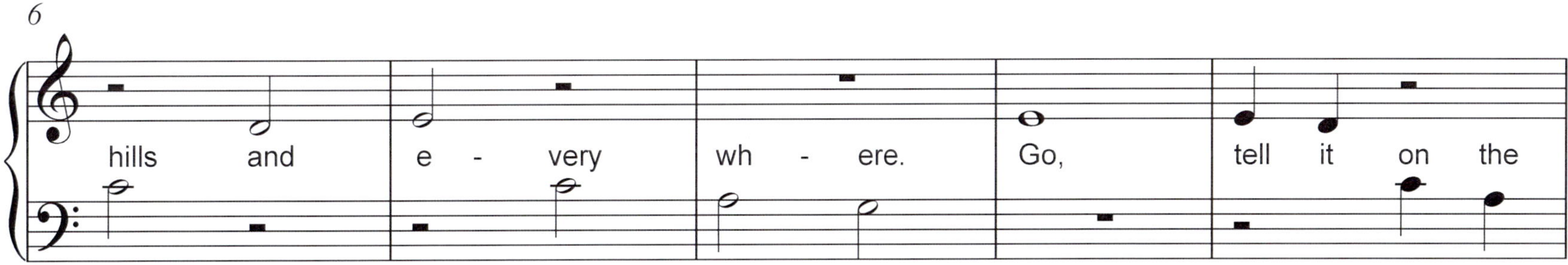
6
hills and e - very wh - ere. Go, tell it on the

11
moun - tain, that Je - sus Christ is born!

Bring a Torch Jeanette, Isabella

Softly

Traditional

5
p
Bring a torch Jea - nette, Is - a - bella - a
1

5
Bring a torch to - the cr - a - dle run.

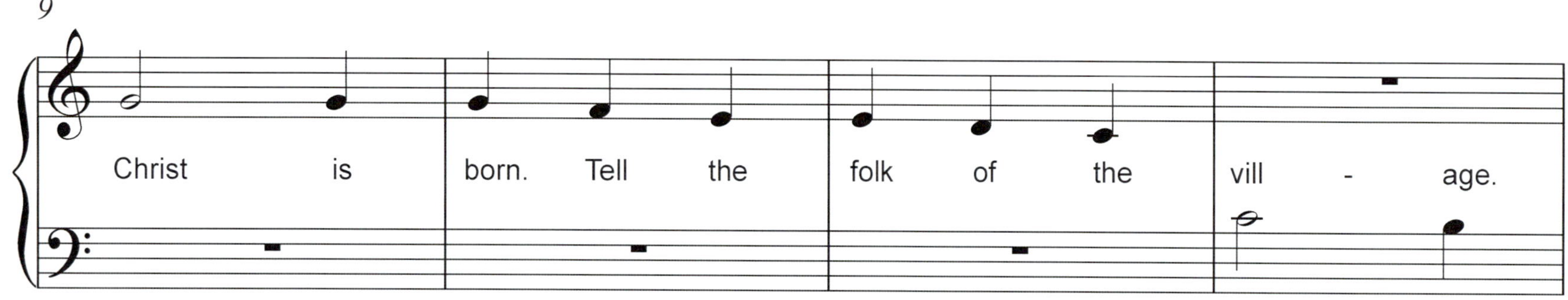
9
Christ is born. Tell the folk of the vill - age.

13
Je - sus is born and Ma - ry's call - ing.

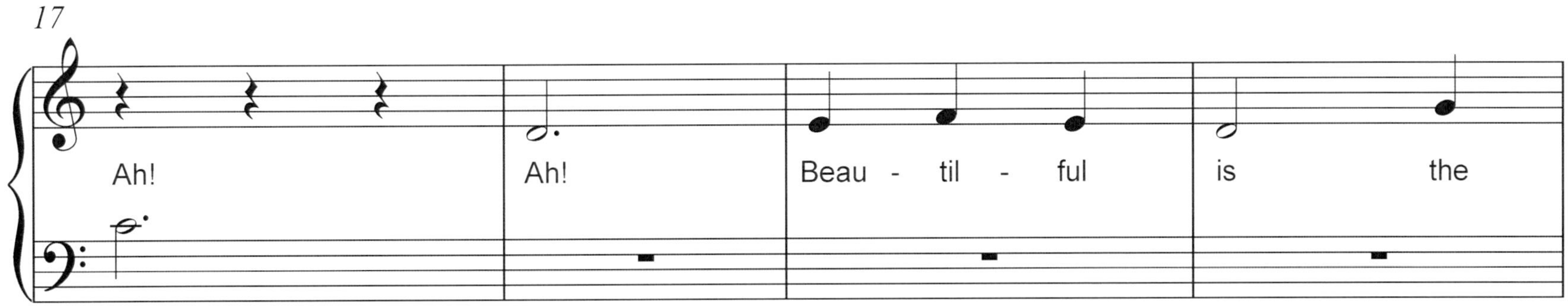
17
Ah! Ah! Beau - til - ful is the

21
moth - er. Ah! Ah! Beau - ti - ful is her child.

www.ingramcontent.com/pod-product-compliance
Ingram Content Group UK Ltd.
Pitfield, Milton Keynes, MK11 3LW, UK
UKRC032309290726
14090UKWH00004B/402

* 9 7 9 8 9 8 5 0 8 8 1 0 6 *